ASSURANCE

40 DAYS
OF
ASSURANCE

In-depth personal reflections that add surety to your convictions that God is faithful so that you may know the peace that passes all understanding.

Rita Kroon

Seek the Lord to fill your empty cup with your daily portion that you may be strengthened in your faith.

A Walk to the Well

Assurance

As the purple crocuses in the snow
give winter-weary people the assurance
that spring is coming, so it is with the
Gospel of Jesus Christ that gives assurance
to sin-stained people that He paid the
sin debt and calls us to believe
unto eternal life.

Dedication

In loving memory of my husband, Burt,
and our daughter, Rene'
my other two daughters, LaDawn and Shelly,
their husbands and children,
My sister, Gayle, and
to all who have ever needed
assurance of being loved some time
in their lives, may I give you the
assurance that Jesus loves you immensely!

Rita Kroon

Table of Contents

DAY 1 ~ EDIFY OUR NEIGHBOR 1

DAY 2 ~ CHILDREN OF GOD 3

DAY 3 ~ RECONCILED TO GOD...5

DAY 4 ~ ETERNAL LIFE 7

DAY 5 ~ SETTING THE MIND ON THE SPIRIT 9

DAY 6 ~ PRAYER WITHOUT DISSENSION 11

DAY 7 ~ TO KNOW CHRIST 13

DAY 8 ~ HAVE LOVE, KNOW LOVE...............................15

DAY 9 ~ TRUE SPIRITUAL WORSHIP 17

DAY 10 ~ ABIDE FOREVER...19

DAY 11 ~ POWER OF THE CROSS.....................................21

DAY 12 ~ NO FEAR OF THOSE WHO KILL.....................23

DAY 13 ~ BELIEF UNTO SALVATION 25

DAY 14 ~ WALK IN A WORTHY MANNER.......................27

DAY 15 ~ WISDOM LEADING TO SALVATION 29

DAY 16 ~ PROVE TO BE BLAMELESS 31

DAY 17 ~ TO BEAR FRUIT..33

DAY 18 ~ CLOTHED IN RIGHTEOUSNESS 35

DAY 19 ~ VICTORY OVER SIN & DEATH 37

DAY 20 ~ LOVE WITHOUT HYPOCRISY 39

DAY 21 ~ FULFILL THE LAW THROUGH LOVE 41

DAY 22 ~ EQUIPPED FOR EVERY GOOD WORK.................43

DAY 23 ~ STAND AGAINST EVIL SCHEMES 45

DAY 24 ~ ETERNAL LIFE..47

DAY 25 ~ LOVE ONE ANOTHER 49

DAY 26 ~ BE ANXIOUS FOR NOTHING 51

DAY 27 ~ BELIEVE UNTO ETERNAL LIFE.......................53

DAY 28 ~ SALVATION 55

DAY 29 ~ KNOWLEDGE OF GOD'S MYSTERY.................57

DAY 30 ~ HOPE IN TROUBLED TIMES.................................59
DAY 31 ~ CONVINCED OF TRUTH.....................................61
DAY 32 ~ FROM DEATH TO LIFE.......................................63
DAY 33~ SANCTIFICATION 65
DAY 34 ~ LEAD A QUIET LIFE...67
DAY 35 ~ REIGN WITH CHRIST...69
DAY 36 ~ MIND SET ON HOLINESS 71
DAY 37 ~ HELP IN TIME OF NEED.....................................73
DAY 38 ~ KNOW EVERLASTING LOVE 75
DAY 39 ~ WALK BY FAITH 77
DAY 40 ~ BE TRANSFORMED 79
MEET THE AUTHOR...84
OTHER BOOKS BY RITA KROON 86

Introduction

May this be your expectation every morning as you bring your empty cup before the Lord: that He would fill your cup with your **daily portion** from His Word that you may drink deeply and be nourished. *Lord, You have assigned me my portion and my cup. You have made my lot secure. Psalm 16:5*

Each day has a key verse for the topic at hand, but also includes passages to read before and after the selected verse in order to reveal its meaning within the context of Scripture. The **goal** of the passage of Scripture becomes clear, along with the **obstacles** that stand in the way of attaining the goal, **affirmations** that reinforce the truth of God's Word, a **personal application of the principles,** and the **Result** where you will be able to determine if your Result coincide with the goal of the passage. Two personal questions follow that you ask yourself in order to prayerfully examine your heart to determine if you are reaching your goal and what it is that may be hindering you.

Assurance inspires confidence much like a guarantee gives freedom from doubt, an unconditional commitment to the belief that something will happen or that something is true. When one is assured of something, that one is made confident in their belief and cannot be swayed by falsehood. Assurance gives confidence and the surety of what was said to be truthful and trustworthy.

Do you have doubts about your walk with God? Insecure with parenting skills? A lack of confidence in who you are? Fear of the future? Indecisive? Anxiety with health issues? Troubled with a myriad of other areas of concern? Sometimes we just need to have loving arms around us to assure us that everything will work out or, we may just need to be affirmed that we are loved. Whatever the reason, be assured. You are not abandoned. You are not alone. This collection of forty daily devotionals will guide you to reach that needed surety of your convictions that God is faithful. Discover the peace that passes all understanding as you bring your empty cup to the Lord that He may fill it with your daily portion of His grace. Come, drink deeply of God's word that you may find assurance through His strength.

Fill your cup with your daily portion as a
day-by-day reminder of our
dependence on Jesus.

Fill your cup and be satisfied in
the Lord Jesus Christ.

Day 1~ Edify Our Neighbor

Read Romans 15:1-6

Rom. 15:1-2 *"We who are strong have an obligation to bear with the failings of the weak, and not to please ourselves. ²Let each of us please his neighbor for his good, to build him up."* (ESV)

Goal: To edify our neighbor for his good.

Obstacles: Eating certain foods that may cause someone to stumble, putting too much emphasis on eating and drinking thereby diminishing the testimony of the kingdom of God, causing dissension by what is eaten or drunk, tearing down the work of God for the sake of food, and doubting one's own conviction of faith.

Affirmations: Paul states in his letter to the Romans that even Christ did not please Himself. Through perseverance and the encouragement of the Scriptures, we have hope. God gives us perseverance and encouragement that we need.

Personal Application of the Principles: We must be careful we do not become a stumbling block to another's belief in Christ by what we may or may not eat or drink. We dare not cause another to stumble by our actions. We receive perseverance and encouragement from God which strengthens us in our hope.

Result: We are able to build up our neighbors.

<u>Ask yourself</u>: How can I sincerely delight in building up my neighbor?

If others were to observe me, what would they say is my greatest stumbling block to others?

Day 2 ~ Children of God

Read John 1:6-13

John 1:12-13 *"But to all who did receive Him, who believed in His name, He gave the right to become children of God, ¹³who were born, not of blood nor of the will of the flesh nor of the will of man, but of God."* (ESV)

Goal: To become children of God.

Obstacles: God is spirit and man cannot see God in His essence (His Spirit-being), the world did not believe in the Word, the world received Him not, and man is human and cannot connect to the Spirit without a link.

Affirmations: John says very plainly that the Word became flesh, He dwelt among man, He made man, He enlightens man, He came to reconcile man with God, and He has power to give those who believe the right to be called children of God. Jesus is the only begotten from the Father, and grace and truth were realized though Jesus.

Personal Application of the Principles: Since we know the truth that man is separated from God by our sinful, human natures, we realize that we need a connecting link to reconcile us to God and that link is the Light of the world, namely Jesus Christ, the only begotten Son of God who is full of grace and truth. The spirit of man must be born again in order to be connected to God – a holy and righteous Spirit being.

Result: We are assured that if we are born again, we are called children of God.

<u>Ask yourself</u>: How did I come to receive Jesus, that is, to believe in His name?

Why is rejoicing a natural response to being a child of God?

Day 3 ~ Reconciled to God

Read 2 Corinthians 5:14-21

2 Cor. 5:17 *"Therefore, if any man is in Christ, he is a new creature, the old things passed away, behold, new things have come."*

Goal: To be reconciled to God

Obstacles: Sin nature, wicked hearts, inability to reach holiness in ourselves, and the impossibility to free ourselves from sin.

Affirmations: Paul explains that Christ died on our behalf by taking all our sins upon Himself on the cross. He rose again in victory over sin, death, and the penalty for sin. Man is a new creation, and his old sin nature is made new. God in Christ reconciled the world to Himself which means He does not count our sins against us. We are free to be His ambassadors to others when we become the righteousness of God in Jesus.

Personal Application of the Principles: God in Christ works in our old sin nature to cleanse us from sin that we may be reconciled to God. It is not in our own strength or of our own will, but because of God's immense love for us. We are new creatures since our old sin nature is gone. Because God does not count our sins against us, we become the righteousness of God in Jesus, and we are free to be His ambassadors to others.

Result: We are reconciled to God.

Ask yourself: What is my greatest obstacle for reconciliation with God, and how do I overcome it?

How can I be sure I am reconciled to God?

Day 4 ~ Eternal Life

Read Matthew 19:16-26

Matt. 19:26 *"And looking upon them Jesus said, 'With men this is impossible, but with God all things are possible.'"*

Goal: To have eternal life

Obstacles: Breaking the commandments if one wants to live under the Law and striving for perfection in self, thereby, not seeing the need for a Savior, and thinking that good works can gain salvation. Pride, selfishness, trusting in riches, and trying to be good enough.

Affirmations: Matthew says that there is only One who is good, and that if anyone could keep the whole Law perfectly, he could gain heaven. Jesus knows our sinful hearts and He sees our need, and that with God all things are possible through faith in Jesus and not through works of man.

Personal Application of the Principles: When we realize our sinfulness, we have taken our first step towards salvation. We must let go of all earthly things – especially riches if we were to put our trust in them for eternal life. We dare not hold anything earthly more dearly than Christ Jesus. Salvation is only possible with God since He holds the key to the door of heaven and only through Jesus can we have access to eternal life.

Result: Eternal life

Ask yourself: How do I know I have eternal life?

Why is eternal life not possible if it were dependent upon me?

Day 5 ~ Setting the Mind on the Spirit

Read Romans 8:1-11

Rom. 8:6 *"For the mind set on the flesh is death, but the mind set on the Spirit is life and peace."*

Goal: To learn to set the mind on the Spirit

Obstacles: The flesh is weak, the Law cannot set man free, a sinful nature, minds set on the things of the flesh, immorality, impurity, sensuality, idolatry, sorcery, enmities, strife, jealousy, anger, disputes, dissensions, factions, envy, drunkenness, carousing, and hostility toward God.

Affirmations: Paul points out that what man could not do, God did by sending His Son as an offering for sin. God condemned sin in the flesh, and man has been set free from the mindset of fleshly desires so that we are able to set our minds on the Spirit. The Spirit of God indwells believers, and our spirit is alive because of His righteousness.

Personal Application of the Principles: We know that what we could not do, God did through Jesus Christ who gave Himself as an offering for our sin. We have been set free from the mindset of fleshly desires. The Spirit of God dwells in us, and our spirits are alive because of His righteousness.

Result: We are able to set our minds on the Spirit.

<u>Ask yourself</u>: What distractions keep me from setting my mind on the Spirit?

How do I overcome my weak flesh?

Day 6 ~ Prayer without Dissension

Read 1 Timothy 2:1-8

1 Tim. 2:5 *"For there is one God and one Mediator between God and men, the Man Christ Jesus who gave Himself as a ransom for all, the testimony born at the proper time."* (ESV)

Goal: To strive to have prayer without wrath or dissension

Obstacles: Lack of knowledge of the truth, prayers said with dissension, petitions said with no connection to God, prayers asked without godliness and dignity, and lack of godly prayers asked on behalf of others, especially for those who are in government authority.

Affirmations: In his letter to Timothy, Paul states clearly that Christ Jesus is the only Mediator between God and man, and He gave Himself as a ransom for all. Jesus gives faith and restores man, He frees man from dissension, and He makes truth known to man. God expresses His wish (not His decree) that all men would be saved and to come to the knowledge of the truth.

Personal Application of the Principles: When we are reconciled to God through the death of Jesus Christ, we have purity of life, and our prayers will be heard. If we have dissension with another, God does not hear our prayers. We know that God wishes all men to be saved – to come to the knowledge of the truth.

Result: We are enabled to pray, putting aside all wrath and dissension.

<u>Ask yourself</u>: Why is dissension with another a hindrance to effective prayer?

How can my prayers be considered effective prayers if I don't see my prayers answered?

Day 7 ~ To Know Christ

Read Philippians 3:1-11

Phil. 3:7-8 *"But whatever gain I had, I counted as loss for the sake of Christ. ⁸Indeed, I count everything as loss because of the surpassing worth of knowing Christ Jesus, my Lord. For His sake I have suffered the loss of all things and count them as rubbish, in order that I may gain Christ."* (ESV)

Goal: To know Christ and the power of His resurrection

Obstacles: Confidence in the flesh, legalism, dependence on heritage as a way of salvation, and being zealous for the wrong reason, and with wrong motives.

Affirmations: Paul writes to the Philippians that believers worship in the Spirit of God and glory in Jesus Christ. Believers put no confidence in the flesh, that all things of the flesh are counted as rubbish compared to faith and a right relationship with Christ. Believers can know Christ and can be found righteous in Him through faith. and there is power in the resurrection of Jesus.

Personal Application of the Principles: We cannot trust in our own credentials to know Christ Jesus as our Lord. We must come to Him in faith in who He is and the power He has.

Result: We put Jesus ahead of everything else which means to love Him with all our hearts.

<u>Ask yourself</u>: How can I love Christ whom I have not seen over my family whom I see?

What is the power of Christ's resurrection to me, and what wrong motives could prevent me from experiencing that power?

Day 8 ~ Have Love, Know Love

Read 1 Corinthians 13:1-13

1 Cor. 13:13 *"But now abide faith, hope, love, these three, but the greatest of these is love."*

Goal: To have love, and to know love

Obstacles: Preoccupation with spiritual gifts, focus on giving to the poor as a saving work, and any task done outside of love.

Affirmations: Paul tenderly explains that love is patient and kind, is not jealous, does not brag and is not arrogant. Love does not act unbecomingly and is not selfish, it is not easily provoked, nor does it consider a wrong suffered, it does not rejoice in unrighteousness, but rejoices with truth. Love bears all things, hopes all things, endures all things, and even though Spiritual gifts and knowledge will cease, love never fails.

Personal Application of the Principles: We strive to have love – to know what love really is. We know in part now, but we will be fully known, and when we see Jesus face to face, we will know love in its fullest essence because God is love. We cannot focus on good works or gifts given to us at the exclusion of love.

Result: We will have love, and we will know love.

Ask yourself: How can I love others if I doubt God's love for me?

With what am I most preoccupied, and how can I re-focus on loving God with my whole heart and others as myself?

Day 9 ~ True Spiritual Worship

Read Romans 11:33-12:2

Rom. 12:1-2 *"I urge you therefore, brothers, by the mercies of God to present your bodies as a living sacrifice, holy and acceptable to God, which is your spiritual worship. [12]Do not be conformed to this world, but be transformed by the renewal of your mind, that by testing you may discern what is the will of God: what is good and acceptable and perfect."* (ESV)

Goal: To have true spiritual worship through which we can discern the will of God.

Obstacles: Conforming to the world and false worship.

Affirmations: Paul urges his readers to know that the depth of both the wisdom and knowledge of God makes His judgments unsearchable and His ways inscrutable. No one has known the mind of God, and no one can give to God that He might be repaid because all things are from Him, through Him, and to Him. Therefore, God alone is worthy of worship.

Personal Application of the Principles: We are to present our bodies as a living and holy sacrifice which is our spiritual worship meaning that we are not to be conformed to this world but to be renewed in our minds which transforms us and enables us to discern the perfect will of God.

Result: We have true spiritual worship and are then able to discern God's will.

Ask yourself: Why should I not be conformed to this world?

What does it mean to worship in spirit and truth?

Day 10 ~ Abide Forever

Read 1 John 2:12-17

1 John 2:15-17 *"Do not love the world or the things in the world. If anyone loves the world, the love of the Father is not in him. ¹⁶For all that is in the world: the lust of the flesh, the lust of the eyes and the pride of life, is not from the Father, but is of the world. ¹⁷And the world is passing away along with its lusts, but he who does the will of God abides forever."* (NKJV)

Goal: To abide forever

Obstacles: Loving worldly possessions above God, lust of the flesh, lust of the eyes, and the pride of life.

Affirmations: John assures us that our sins are forgiven, that God can be known, that believers have overcome the evil one, that the word of God abides in believers, and the world with its lusts is passing away.

Personal Application of the Principles: We are to love God above all worldly possessions. We are not to lust after things in this life. We are to put away pride and obey the Father in all things. The word of God abides in us so we can be strong in our faith.

Result: We will overcome the evil one, and we will abide forever.

Ask yourself: How can I know the will of God and what does it mean to me to do the will of God?

How does obeying the will of God help me to overcome the evil one?

Day 11 ~ Power of the Cross

Read 1 Corinthians 1:10-21

1 Cor. 1:18 *"For the word of the cross is folly to those who are perishing, but to us who are being saved it is the power of God."* (ESV)

Goal: To have belief in the power of the cross unto salvation

Obstacles: Dissension among believers, looking at man above Jesus, trusting in man's wisdom to know God, unbelief, and worldly wisdom that cannot understand the power of the cross.

Affirmations: Paul emphasizes that the word of the cross is the power of God for believers, and that God made foolish the wisdom of the world. God was well-pleased through the "foolishness" of the message preached to save those who believe, and that there should be no distinction among preachers that one is better than another. The cross of Christ is not made void, but it is the power of God for salvation.

Personal Application of the Principles: We should not think more highly of ourselves if we attend a certain church with its minister over another church or pastor, but rather, put aside all dissension and strive for unity as long as the truth is upheld and we are of the same mind who believe in the cross of Christ.

Result: We believe that the cross of Christ is the power of God unto salvation.

Ask yourself: Why did God choose the cross to display His power, and how have I experienced the power of the cross?

Why is trusting in the finished work of Jesus Christ on the cross better than trusting in my good works?

Day 12 ~ No Fear of those who Kill the Body

Read Matthew 10:16-33

Matt. 10:28 *"And do not fear those who kill the body but are not able to kill the soul, rather fear Him who is able to destroy both body and soul in hell."* (ESV)

Goal: To fear not those who can kill the body.

Obstacles: Man delivers others over to the courts, brother delivers brother to death, hated by all, fear, denial of Christ under persecution, and satanic influence.

Affirmations: Matthew assures believers that testimony will be given them at the time of need, that whoever endures to the end will be saved, that Jesus will come again, that sins of the enemy will be found out, that man is not able to kill the soul, and that the Father knows of our tribulations and cares deeply. God values believers more than anything on earth, and if believers confess Jesus before men, Jesus will confess us before His Father.

Personal Application of the Principles: We need not be anxious what we should say during perilous times of the testimony of Jesus because He told us these things would happen. As we endure persecutions, we can look up in the hope of Jesus' soon return. Since God is sovereign, we can be encouraged to know that He cares deeply about us, and that He will deliver us. Therefore, we must not deny Christ out of fear of rejection by others.

Result: We need not fear those who can kill the body but are unable to kill the soul.

<u>Ask yourself:</u> Since fear of danger from another human being is natural for all humanity, how do I put away fear of harm or death from another person?

How can I transfer fear of man to trust in Christ??

Day 13 ~ Belief unto Salvation

Read Acts 4:1-14

Acts: 4:12 *"And there is salvation in no one else, for there is no other name under heaven given among men by which we must be saved." ESV*

Goal: To believe in the name of Jesus unto salvation.

Obstacles: Persecution, false teachers, evil rulers, false doctrine in churches, legalism, and unbelief.

Affirmations: Luke points out that when the disciples proclaimed the resurrection from the dead, 5000 believed that God raised Jesus from the dead. The disciples healed in Jesus' name. There is salvation in no other name under heaven, and those who believe in the name of Jesus will be saved. Peter and John spoke with confidence and boldness of the healing and saving power of Jesus since they were eyewitnesses of Jesus' resurrection.

Personal Application of the Principles: We cannot believe in Jesus and yet, reject the reality of His resurrection since His resurrection was tangible proof that Jesus is the Christ and that there is salvation in no other. False teachers and evil leaders will always be, but we can have faith that they are only temporary. Our actions speak volumes of our belief in the saving power in the name of Jesus Christ.

25

Result: We believe in the name of Jesus Christ for salvation.

Ask yourself: How did I come to believe in the name of Jesus Christ for my salvation?

What is my greatest assurance of eternal life?

Day 14 ~ Walk in a Worthy Manner

Read Colossians 1:3-14

Col. 1:9-10 *"For this reason also, since the day we heard of it, we have not ceased to pray for you and to ask that you may be filled with the knowledge of His will in all spiritual wisdom and understanding [10]so that you may walk in a manner worthy of the Lord..."*

Goal: To walk in a manner worthy of the Lord.

Obstacles: Lack of knowledge and understanding, unbelief, spiritual weakness, impatience, stoic demeanor, darkness and evil, and sin and unforgiveness.

Affirmations: Paul writes of the faith in Jesus Christ that will enable believers to love others because of the hope of heaven. Bearing fruit comes with understanding the grace of God in truth. Believers are filled with the knowledge of His will in all spiritual wisdom and are strengthened with power. Believers are delivered from the domain of darkness and are transferred to the kingdom of Jesus giving believers redemption and forgiveness of sins.

Personal Application of the Principles: Our faith in Jesus Christ will enable us to love others since we have hope laid up for us in heaven. We have the word of truth and will bear fruit that comes with hearing and understanding the grace of

God. We strive to please Him in all respects, bearing fruit in every good work, and increasing in the knowledge of God.

Result: We can walk in a manner worthy of the Lord and please Him in all respects bearing fruit in every good work.

Ask yourself: How am I walking in a manner worthy of the Lord?

What does that mean to me?

Day 15 ~ Wisdom Leading to Salvation

Read 2 Timothy 3:1-17

2 Tim. 3:15 *"...and that from childhood you have known the sacred writings which are able to give you the wisdom that leads to salvation through faith which is in Christ Jesus."*

Goal: To have wisdom that leads to salvation through faith in Christ Jesus and to be adequately equipped for every good work.

Obstacles: Difficult times, love of money, selfishness, pride, rebellion, disobedience, ungrateful heart, sin, gossip, religion and not faith, impulsiveness, lack of knowledge of truth, rejection of faith, and persecution.

Affirmations: Paul states that believers persevere in truth and are taught truth in Scripture, that salvation is through faith in Jesus Christ alone, and that wisdom comes through the word of God, that all Scripture is inspired by God and is profitable for teaching, reproof, correction, and for training in righteousness.

Personal Application of the Principles: No matter what difficult times or persecution surrounds us, we have been taught the truth in Scripture. We gain wisdom by studying God's word which teaches that salvation is through faith in Jesus Christ. We can trust the Scriptures because they are the inspired word of God. We can use Scripture for teaching, for reproof, for correction, and for training in righteousness.

Result: We have the faith through wisdom that leads to salvation and will be equipped for every good work in Christ Jesus.

<u>Ask yourself</u>: Do I have the wisdom that leads to salvation through the necessary faith in Christ Jesus, and if so, where does my assurance come from?

How can I encourage others to seek such wisdom?

Day 16 ~ Prove to be Blameless

Read Philippians 2:12-16

Phil. 2:14-15 *"Do all things without grumbling or disputing, [15]that you may prove yourselves to be blameless and innocent, children of God above reproach in the midst of a crooked and perverse generation, among whom you appear as lights in the world."*

Goal: To prove to be blameless, innocent, and above reproach

Obstacles: Disobedience, pride, grumbling or disputing, and living in a perverse generation.

Affirmations: Paul writes that it is God who works in us to will and to work for His good pleasure, to prove yourselves to be blameless and innocent children of God above reproach in the midst of a crooked and perverse generation, that we appear as lights in the world and to hold fast the word of life, and that we should so live that we would reflect the light that comes from heaven, namely Jesus Christ.

Personal Application of the Principles: As believers, we seek to do God's will knowing that it is God who works in us for His good pleasure so that we may prove to be blameless and innocent in the midst of a perverse generation. We are as lights in a dark world if we hold fast to the word of God in Christ Jesus.

31

Result: We will prove to be blameless and innocent for His glory.

Ask yourself: How am I made blameless and innocent in the eyes of men and before a Holy God?

How does God work in me to be a light in a dark, chaotic world?

Day 17 ~ To Bear Fruit

Read John 15:1-12

John 15:5 *"I am the vine, you are the branches, whoever abides in me and I in him, he it is that bears much fruit, for apart from Me you can do nothing."* (ESV)

Goal: To bear spiritual fruit

Obstacles: Disobedience.

Affirmations: John says that apart from Jesus, we can do nothing, and those who do not abide in Jesus are cast out. If we abide in Jesus and His words abide in us, we can ask for whatever we wish and it will be given us. If we keep His commandments, we will abide in His love and will produce fruit. His commandment is to love one another.

Personal Application of the Principles: If we abide/remain in Jesus, we will pray with the mind of Christ and therefore, will only ask for those things that He desires, and our prayers will be answered. If we abide in Jesus and His words abide in us, we will obey His commandment to love one another.

Result: We will produce spiritual fruit, which is love, joy, peace, patience, kindness, goodness, faithfulness, gentleness, and self-control.

Ask yourself: How am I bearing fruit?

What do I need in order to pray effective prayers?

Day 18 ~ Clothed in Righteousness

Read 1 John 2:28-3:4

1 John 3:1 *"See how great a love the Father has bestowed upon us that we should be called children of God, and such we are."*

Goal: To be children of God clothed in righteousness.

Obstacles: Sin, lawlessness, unrighteousness, guilt, shame.

Affirmations: John's letter says that Jesus is righteous and everyone who practices righteousness is born of Him. When He appears, we may have confidence and not shrink back in shame, for the Father loves us with so great a love that He would call us children of God. When He appears, we shall be like Him, we shall see Him as He is. Therefore, we are to fix our hope on Him and to purify ourselves just as He is pure.

Personal Application of the Principles: Because Jesus is righteous, we can practice righteousness since we are born of God. We have confidence in our righteousness through Him. Therefore, we do not have to shrink back in shame. We are called children of God. We fix our hope on Jesus and purify ourselves just as He is pure.

Result: We are children of God clothed in His righteousness.

<u>Ask yourself</u>: How can I be assured that I am a child of God?

What is the one thing that prevents anyone from being a child of God?

Day 19 ~ Victory Over Sin & Death

Read 1 Corinthians 15:51-58

1 Cor. 15: 56-57 *"The sting of death is sin, and the power of sin is the law, [57]but thanks be to God who gives us the victory through our Lord Jesus Christ."*

Goal: Victory over sin and death

Obstacles: Mortal man, sin, death, weak faith, and easily led astray.

Affirmations: Paul writes with assurance that we will all be changed, the perishable must put on the imperishable, the mortal must put on immortality, death will lose its sting and its victory, sin will be no more because it is by sin that death gains authority over man and the power of sin is the Law because the Law stirs up sin, and that God gives us victory through our Lord Jesus Christ.

Personal Application of the Principles: We believe from God's word that we will obtain victory over sin and death through our Lord Jesus Christ. We are enabled to abound in every good work of the Lord. We know our toil will not be in vain. We know we will be changed from mortal to immortal and death will be defeated. Death will have no authority over us.

Result: We will have victory over sin and death.

Ask yourself: How can I know that I have victory over sin and death?

What is my greatest obstacle for knowing such a victory while on earth?

Day 20 ~ Love Without Hypocrisy

Read Romans 12:9-21

Rom. 12:9 *"Let love be without hypocrisy."*

Goal: To love all people without hypocrisy.

Obstacles: Evil, selfishness, lack of zeal, hopelessness, tribulation, persecution, no compassion, haughtiness, prejudice, vengeance, disrespect of what is right, and quarrelsome.

Affirmations: Paul encourages us to be devoted to one another, to hate evil and to cling to what is good, to give preference to others in honor, to serve the Lord with diligence and fervency in the Spirit, to rejoice in hope, to persevere in tribulation, to be devoted in prayer, to contribute to the needs of others, to be hospitable, to bless those who persecute, to show compassion and joy, to show no prejudice, to respect what is right, to be at peace with all men as much as possible, to respect what is right, to not take revenge, and to overcome evil with good.

Personal Application of the Principles: As believers, we are to strive to be devoted to other believers, to honor them, and to contribute to the needs of others with a glad heart. We are encouraged to show hospitality to all. We pray to hate evil, put away selfishness, and to love what is good. We look to serve the Lord diligently, to show compassion, and to have joy. We are to let peace reign in our hearts and take no revenge against others.

Result: We will love others with genuine love, that is, without any hypocrisy.

<u>Ask yourself</u>: How do I know if my love for others is genuine?

What obstacle must I overcome to have genuine love?

Day 21 ~ Fulfill the Law through Love

Read Rom. 13:8-14

Rom. 13:8 *"Owe nothing to anyone except to love one another, for he who loves his neighbor has fulfilled the law."*

Goal: To fulfill the Law through love

Obstacles: Debt, hate, adultery, murder, theft, covetousness, deeds of darkness, lust, carousing, drunkenness, promiscuity, sensuality, strife and jealousy.

Affirmations: Paul tells us that he who loves his neighbor has fulfilled the Law, love your neighbor as yourself, love does no wrong, love is the fulfillment of the Law, that salvation is nearer than when we first believed, to put on the armor of light, and to put on the Lord Jesus Christ.

Personal Application of the Principles: We can overcome the deeds of darkness by putting on the armor of light which is the word of truth in the power of God. We can put on the Lord Jesus Christ, and if so, we will be able to love our neighbors as ourselves. If we walk in Jesus' love, and have true and genuine love, we will do no wrong to our neighbors.

Result: We will love our neighbors as ourselves and thereby, fulfill the Law. We will do only good to our neighbors for their benefit.

Ask yourself: Why does love fulfill the Law, and am I still under the Law?

How do I use the Word of Truth to overcome the deeds of darkness?

Day 22 ~ Equipped for Every Good Work

Read 2 Timothy 3:10-17

2 Tim. 3:12, 15, 17 *"And indeed, all who desire to live godly in Christ Jesus will be persecuted."* ¹⁵*"...and that from childhood you have known the sacred writings which are able to give you the wisdom that leads to salvation through faith which is in Christ Jesus."* ¹⁷*"...that the man of God may be adequate, equipped for every good work."*

Goal: To live a godly life in Christ Jesus, and to be adequately equipped for every good work

Obstacles: False teachings, misconduct, unbelief, impatience, hate, persecution, suffering, evil men, imposters, deceivers, and apostasy.

Affirmations: Paul wishes Timothy to follow his example, since he had the Scriptures which are able to give wisdom that leads to salvation through faith in Jesus Christ, and to realize that all Scripture is inspired by God and is profitable for teaching, for reproof, for correction, and for training in righteousness so that the man of God would be adequately equipped for every good work.

Personal Application of the Principles: Believers, godly people who follow the teaching of Scripture, can expect to be persecuted. Qualities of godly people include good conduct, faith, patience, love and perseverance. Christians believe

43

that Scripture is the inspired word of God, that it is able to give wisdom unto salvation, and to fully equip us for good works.

Result: We are fully equipped for every good work.

<u>Ask yourself</u>: What does living a godly life look like to me?

What is my greatest deterrent to doing good works, and are good works necessary for salvation?

Day 23 ~ Stand Against Evil Schemes

Read Ephesians 6:10-18

Eph. 6:11 *"Put on the whole armor of God that you may be able to stand against the schemes of the devil."* (ESV)

Goal: To stand against the schemes of the devil

Obstacles: Demonic hosts of Satan assembled for mortal battle, the rulers, authorities and world forces of evil, spiritual forces of evil in the heavenly places, not prepared to stand against the devil, no faith, not grounded in the Word.

Affirmations: In his letter to the Ephesians, Paul says to put on the full armor of God, that God's armor is spiritual armor to combat spiritual evil forces, that we have the truth, righteousness, gospel, faith, salvation, word of God, prayer, and the Holy Spirit, to be alert and to persevere.

Personal Application of the Principles: We are made aware of Satan's tactics and are provided with the armor (righteousness, the gospel, faith, our salvation, the word of God, prayer, and the Holy Spirit) to combat him through the truth in God's Word.

Result: We are fully equipped, therefore we can stand firm against the evil schemes of the devil.

Ask yourself: How can I be fully equipped to stand against the schemes of the devil, and do I stand on my own against the devil?

What is my greatest weapon to stand against evil schemes, and how do I use it?

Day 24 ~ Eternal Life

Read Mark 10:17-31

Mark 10:17 *"And as He was setting out on a journey, a man ran up to Him and knelt before Him and began asking Him, 'Good Teacher, what shall I do to inherit eternal life?'"*

Goal: To obtain eternal life

Obstacles: Sin, unbelief, love of material things, money, and riches above God, trusting in wealth, and man's efforts to gain eternal life through good works.

Affirmations: Mark writes Jesus' response that 'No one is good except God.' In essence, Jesus is saying He is God in the flesh. Jesus then said that the man must keep the commandments perfectly if he was to have eternal life. Jesus knew the man was a good man by human standards, but he was not perfect by God's standards. That is why Jesus came to take our place on the cross to pay the penalty for all sin, and that one has eternal life by grace through faith and not by good works lest anyone should boast. The commandments are a guide to what sins are, that sins of the heart are as deadly as physical actions, that eternal life is not gained through man's efforts, and that those who love God more than anything or anyone will be rewarded in the age to come.

Personal Application of the Principles: Our sins are obstacles against us for gaining eternal life and so is dependence on wealth as well as trying to keep the commandments. God's plan of salvation is to know Jesus Christ, to believe in Him, and to follow Jesus with a heart cleansed by His death on the cross, not by anything we may have or may not have done. God give those who believe in Jesus the right to be called children of God and heirs of eternal live.

Result: Eternal life

Ask yourself: Who am I trusting in, if not in Jesus Christ, for eternal life and why

How am I assured I have eternal life?

Day 25 ~ Love One Another

Read 1 John 3:9-24

1 John 3:11 *"For this is the message which you have heard from the beginning, that we should love one another."*

Goal: To love one another

Obstacles: Sin, practice of unrighteousness, evil deeds, hatred from the world, hate, murder, hard heart toward those in need, disobedience, and unbelief.

Affirmations: John says that those born of God cannot practice (make a habit of) sin, that whoever practices righteousness and loves his brother is born of God, that we should love one another, that love of the brethren is evidence of being born of God, and that Jesus demonstrated His love for man by laying down His life for humanity. We are to love others who are in need through action and not just in words. Those who keep God's commandment to love one another can have assurance that whatever is asked in prayer will be received. God's greatest commandment is to believe in Jesus, and the second one is to love one another. Those who keep these commandments abide in Him and He in them.

Personal Application of the Principles: If we are born of God, we will not practice sin. Our love for others is a sign by which we can measure our righteousness in God, and if we abide in Jesus and love one another, we know that we will receive whatever we ask for in prayer.

Result: We will love one another

<u>Ask yourself</u>: What does it mean to me to love others as God has loved me?

What is hindering me from obeying God's commandments to love God with my whole being and to love others as He loves us?

Day 26 ~ Be Anxious for Nothing

Read Philippians 4:4-13

Phil. 4:6 *"Be anxious for nothing, but in everything by prayer and supplication with thanksgiving, let your requests be made known to God."*

Goal: To be anxious for nothing

Obstacles: Lack of prayer, wrong thinking, practicing evil, becoming lukewarm, lack of fervency, difficult circumstances, and dependence on self.

Affirmations: Paul states that in everything by prayer and supplication with thanksgiving, let your requests be known to God, that the peace of God, which goes far beyond all understanding, will guard our hearts and minds in Christ Jesus. Strive to train the mind to think on things that are true, honorable, right, pure, lovely, of good repute, anything of excellence and worthy of praise. Practice these things and be an example of them so that you may have the peace of God. Rejoice in the Lord, and learn to be content in every circumstance knowing the secret is that we can do all things through Christ Jesus who strengthens us.

Personal Application of the Principles: We are to be intentional to keep a fervent prayer life with thanksgiving as we seek to train ourselves to practice right thinking on such things that are true, honorable, right, pure, lovely, of good repute, are of excellence and worthy of praise. We do well not to dwell on the negative. We are assured that the peace of God is with us and we can rejoice in the Lord. We purpose to let the peace of God reign in our hearts, our minds, and our spirits.

Result: We will not be anxious.

<u>Ask yourself</u>: Why am I an anxious person?

What do I most often think about, and how do I train my mind to think rightly?

Day 27 ~ Believe unto Eternal Life

Read John 3:9-21

John 3:16-17 *"For God so loved the world that He gave His only begotten Son that whoever believes in Him should not perish but have everlasting life. [17]For God did not send His Son into the world to judge the world, but in order that that world should be saved through Him."* (ESV)

Goal: To have belief in Jesus unto eternal life

Obstacles: Heart closed to understanding the things of God, not receiving the witness of God, unbelief, love of darkness, evil deeds, hate for the light.

Affirmations: John testifies that Jesus bears witness of things He knows and has seen, that the Son of Man descended from heaven and must be crucified for the sins of mankind, that whoever believes in Him may have eternal life, that God loved the world so much that He sent His Son into the world – not to condemn the world but in order that the world may be saved through Him, that those who believe in Jesus will never perish (die without hope), that whoever believes in Jesus is not judged, that Jesus is the only begotten Son of God, that Jesus is the light of the world, and that deeds of righteousness are wrought in God.

Personal Application of the Principles: The righteous believe that Jesus, the only begotten Son of God, descended from heaven, and bears witness to the truth of God that whoever believes in Him shall have eternal life, and will never perish. We can have confidence that Jesus is the One sent by God to be the Savior of the world, and those who believe are not judged nor come under condemnation.

Result: We believe in Jesus unto eternal life.

Ask yourself: What assures me that my belief in Jesus leads to eternal life?

How can I be certain that my sins are forgiven?

Day 28 ~ Salvation

Read 1 Peter 1:1-9

1 Peter 1:3, 9 *"Blessed be the God and Father of our Lord Jesus Christ, who according to His great mercy has caused us to be born again to a living hope through the resurrection of Jesus Christ from the dead." ⁹"...obtaining as the outcome of your faith the salvation of your souls."*

Goal: To have salvation

Obstacles: Unbelief, disobedience, and distressed by various trials.

Affirmations: Peter explains that the elect are chosen according to the foreknowledge of the Father by the consecrated work of the Holy Spirit and sprinkled with the blood of Jesus Christ. We are enabled to obey Christ, and it is His great mercy that has caused us to be born again to a living hope through the resurrection of Jesus Christ to obtain an inheritance preserved in heaven for believers. Believers are protected by the power of God through faith. Trials are meant to test and to prove one's faith resulting in praise and glory, and though believers have not seen Jesus, we can believe in Him with great joy.

Personal Application of the Principles: Since we who have been chosen to salvation according to the foreknowledge of the Father through the work of the Holy Spirit and having been applied to us the redeeming worth of the blood of Jesus Christ, we obey Jesus. Because of God's great mercy, we are born again to a living hope through the resurrection of Jesus from the dead and are protected by the power of God.

Result: We are assured of salvation

Ask yourself: What does it mean to me to be born again?

How have I experienced God's mercy?

Day 29 ~ Knowledge of God's Mystery

Read Colossians 1:15-2:3

Col. 2:2 *"...that their hearts may be encouraged, having been knit together in love, and attaining to all the wealth that comes from the full assurance of understanding, resulting in a true knowledge of God's mystery, that is, Christ Himself."*

Goal: To obtain true knowledge of God's mystery

Obstacles: Alienation from God, hostile in mind, doer of evil deeds, sin, lack of understanding of spiritual matters, and discouragement, strife.

Affirmations: Paul writes that Jesus is the image of the invisible God and all the fullness of God dwells in Him. He was before all things and all things hold together in Him. Jesus is the head of the church on earth. He is the beginning – the first-born to be raised from the dead with a glorified body, He reconciled sinful man to Holy God through His death, and He will present us blameless and beyond reproach to the Father. The mystery of God and the hope of glory, Christ Jesus, hidden from ages past, is revealed to man in these last days, and we are complete in Christ with full assurance of understanding.

Personal Application of the Principles: We can know and trust that Jesus Christ is the image of the invisible God. He is eternal, and all things were made by Him and for Him.

Through His death, we are reconciled to God. We can be confident that Jesus will present us holy and blameless to His Father. Jesus is our hope of glory.

Result: We have a true knowledge of God's revealed mystery – Jesus Christ.

<u>Ask yourself</u>: How did I come to know Jesus Christ?

How do my actions reflect Jesus Christ as my Savior?

Day 30 ~ Hope in Troubled Times

Read 2 Corinthians 4:8-18

2 Cor. 4:17 *"For momentary, light affliction is producing for us an eternal weight of glory far beyond all comparison."* (ESV)

Goal: Hope in troubled times

Obstacles: Afflicted in every way, perplexed, persecuted, struck down, and constant suffering.

Affirmations: Paul reminds us that we are not crushed, nor despairing, we are not forsaken, nor destroyed, that the life of Jesus may be manifested in our mortal flesh, that our physical sufferings are often the means by which spiritual life comes to others, that faith enables us to believe and so speak of the coming resurrection knowing that He who raised Jesus will also raise us, and that God's grace causes the giving of thanks to abound to the glory of God. We do not lose heart because of the momentary, light afflictions on earth since they are really producing an eternal weight of glory beyond all comparison from what is temporary and to what is eternal.

Personal Application of the Principles: We may be afflicted, perplexed, persecuted, and even struck down, but believers are not crushed, nor do we despair. We know these sufferings are only temporary and that we have not been forsaken nor will we be destroyed. We can trust that our sufferings may be the very means God uses to bring spiritual life to others. Therefore, we do not lose heart over the momentary, light affliction that is producing for us an eternal weight of glory.

Result: We have hope in troubled times.

Ask yourself: What causes me to lose hope in troubled times?

How can I share the hope in the lives of others who are in troubled times?

Day 31 ~ Convinced of Truth

Read John 16:7-15

John 16:13 *"But when He, the Spirit of truth, comes, He will guide you into all truth, for He will not speak on His own initiative, but whatever He hears, he will speak, and He will disclose to you what is to come."*

Goal: To be convinced of Truth.

Obstacles: Unbelief, sin, and unrighteousness.

Affirmations: John reiterates the words of Jesus when He said that He would send the Helper - the Holy Spirit who will convict the world concerning sin, righteousness, and judgment. Unbelief is the greatest and most basic sin. Righteousness is evidenced by Jesus' return to the Father, judgment has been pronounced on the ruler of this world, the Spirit of Truth will guide us into all truth and will disclose to us what is to come, and the Holy Spirit will glorify Jesus.

Personal Application of the Principles: We trust that the Holy Spirit will convict men to accept the gospel intelligently, although they may still reject the gospel. We know this means that the Holy Spirit will set forth the truth of the gospel to those who have no conviction of sin, no regard for righteousness, and who pay no attention to warnings of the coming judgment. The Holy Spirit will guide us into all truth and will disclose to us what is to come.

Result: We are convinced of the truth.

Ask yourself: How do I discern the Holy Spirit's prompting from my own thoughts regarding the truth of the gospel?

What are my areas of doubt that need to be dispelled and replaced with truth?

Day 32 ~ From Death to Life

Read 1 John 3:9-18

1 John 3:14 *"We know that we have passed from death to life, because we love the brethren. He who does not love his brother abides in death."*

Goal: To pass from death to life

Obstacles: Sin, unrighteousness, unloving towards the brethren, evil deeds, hatred, and selfishness towards the needy.

Affirmations: John writes that everyone born of God practices righteousness because he abides in God. The obvious difference between children of God and children of the devil is that those who do not practice righteousness or love his brother are of the devil and those who do practice righteousness and love of the brethren are of God. A sign that we have eternal life is that we love one another, and he who does not love his brethren, abides in death. Jesus demonstrated His love for us when He laid down His life for us, and we ought to do the same for our brethren. We are to love in word and truth.

Personal Application of the Principles: Believers do not practice sin because we abide in God, and a sign that we are born of God and have eternal life is that we practice righteousness and love the brethren. We are assured of

Jesus' love for us in the fact that He laid down His life for us.

Result: We have assurance that we pass from death to life.

<u>Ask yourself</u>: If my love for others could be measured, would I be considered a child of God or a child of the devil? Why?

On what am I basing my assurance of passing from death to life?

Day 33~ Sanctification

Read 1 Thessalonians 4:1-8

1 Thess. 4:3 *"For this is the will of God, your sanctification, that is, that you abstain from sexual immorality."*

Goal: To be sanctified

Obstacles: Sexual immorality, lustful passion, transgressing or defrauding a brother, impurity, and rejecting God.

Affirmations: In his letter to the Thessalonians, Paul gives instructions by the authority of Jesus Christ how to walk with God and to be pleasing to Him. The will of God is our sanctification (setting apart in holiness), to possess one's own vessel (body) in sanctification and honor, that the Lord is the avenger in all things, and that God called us to holy living.

Personal Application of the Principles: By the authority of Jesus Christ, we have been instructed as how to walk with God and be pleasing to Him. God's will (desire or purpose) is for our sanctification, that is, our progressive holiness of life. We are to live in such a way that we have self-control over our own bodies, keeping it pure, and with honor. If we've been wronged, we are to remember that the Lord is the avenger. God has called us to purity and holiness, which is our sanctification.

Result: We live sanctified lives.

Ask yourself: How can I live a life of purity?

If others were to observe my lifestyle, would they recognize that my lifestyle is different from the world's way of living and why or why not?

Day 34 ~ Lead a Quiet Life

Read 1 Thessalonians 4:9-12

1 Thess. 4:11 "...*and to make it your ambition to lead a quiet life and attend to your own business, and work with your hands, just as we commanded you.*"

Goal: To lead a quiet life

Obstacles: Undisciplined lifestyle, not working, and acting like busybodies.

Affirmations: Paul writes that we are taught by God how to love one another, to make it a goal to lead a quiet life, to attend to one's own business and to work with one's hands as commanded in order to behave properly towards Christians and non-Christians alike, and not to be in need.

Personal Application of the Principles: As believers, we are taught by God how to love one another. We should aspire, or set as our goal, to lead a quiet, peaceable life, to tend to our own business, and to work for a living without expecting a free handout. If we do so, we will behave properly towards Christians and non-Christians alike.

Result: We will lead a quiet lifestyle in honor.

Ask yourself: Do I lead a quiet life or do I live in such a way as to stir up commotion or dissension? How can learn to lead a quiet and honorable life?

How do I define what it means to love one another?

Day 35 ~ Reign with Christ

Read 1 Thessalonians 4:13-18

1 Thess. 4:14 *"For if we believe that Jesus died and rose again, even so God will bring with Him those who have fallen asleep in Jesus."*

Goal: To reign with Christ

Obstacles: Unbelief in Jesus Christ

Affirmations: Paul reiterates the word of the Lord which says that Jesus died and rose again, and that God will bring with Him those who have fallen asleep in Christ. Those who are alive will not precede those who have died in Jesus. The Lord Himself will descend from heaven with a shout, with a voice of the archangel, and with the trumpet of God and the dead in Christ will rise first, and then those who are alive shall be caught up together in the clouds to meet the Lord. We shall always be with the Lord, and we should comfort one another with these words.

Personal Application of the Principles: We can trust the word of the Lord that says Jesus died and rose again. We have the promised hope that at the sound of a shout, the voice of the archangel, and the trumpet of God, He will bring with Him those believers who have previously died and will meet the Lord in the air, and thus we will always be with Him. These words should be a comfort and an assurance to us.

Result: We will reign with Christ Jesus forever.

<u>Ask yourself</u>: Does the promise that believers will reign with Christ comfort or challenge me and why?

How have I prepared myself to be ready to meet the Lord in the air?

Day 36 ~ Mind Set on Holiness

Read Colossians 2:20-3:7

Col. 3:2-3 *"Set your mind on the things above, not on the things that are on earth. ³For you have died, and your life is hidden with Christ in God."*

Goal: To have a mind set on holiness

Obstacles: Submitting to elementary principles of the world, self-made religion, self-abasement, severe treatment of the body, fleshly indulgences, mind set on earthly things, immorality, impurity, passion, evil desires, greed, idolatry, anger, wrath, malice, slander, abusive speech, and lies.

Affirmations: Paul writes that we have died with Christ to man's elementary principles which have the appearance of wisdom but are only self-made religion and self-abasement. They are worthless against fleshly indulgences and are destined to perish. We are to seek the things that are above where Christ is because we have died to earthly things and our lives are hidden with Christ in God. We are to put aside all things evil in nature that only cause God's wrath and to set our minds on things above.

Personal Application of the Principles: Since we belong to Christ, we no longer are governed by man's elementary and worthless principles of a self-made religion that does nothing to free us from fleshly indulgences, but only keeps us prisoner to man's religious rules. Since our lives are hidden with Christ in God, we are set free to seek the holy things above.

Result: We have a mind set on holiness.

<u>Ask yourself</u>: Why is it important to set my mind on holiness?

What are my greatest enticements that hold me captive to man's religion and religious traditions?

Day 37 ~ Help in Time of Need

Read Hebrews 4:12-16

Heb. 4:16 *"Let us therefore draw near with confidence to the throne of grace, that we may receive mercy and may find grace to help in time of need."*

Goal: To find help in time of need.

Obstacles: Nonconformity to God's word, sin, and unbelief.

Affirmations: The author says that the word of God has the power to reach into the innermost parts of man to judge his thoughts. All things are laid bare before the One to whom we must give an account. Jesus is our high priest who has been tempted in every area that man is tempted (the lust of the flesh, the lust of the eyes, and the pride of life), yet without sin. Therefore, we can approach the throne of grace with confidence that we may receive grace and mercy in our time of need.

Personal Application of the Principles: Believers can know the power of the word of God because it pierces to our very depths and exposes even our thoughts and intentions. We are laid bare before the One to whom we must give an account, but because Jesus is our perfect high priest who was tempted in every area as we are, yet without sin, we can approach the throne of God with assurance that we may receive grace and mercy in time of need.

Result: We receive help in time of need.

Ask yourself: How do I confidently approach the throne of the most high God for help in my times of need?

What allows me to have such assurance?

Day 38 ~ Know Everlasting Love

Read Jeremiah 31:1-6

Jer. 31:3 *"The Lord appeared to him from afar, saying, 'I have loved you with an everlasting love, therefore, I have drawn you with loving-kindness.'"*

Goal: To know everlasting love

Obstacles: Sin and unbelief

Affirmations: Jeremiah records the words of the Lord, "I will be the God of all the families of Israel, and they shall be my people." "I have loved you with an everlasting love. Therefore, I have drawn you with loving-kindness." (Hesed is the Hebrew word for loving-kindness and means loyal, steadfast, faithful love and stresses the idea of belonging together.) Because of the Lord's everlasting love and faithfulness, He will rebuild Israel and they will once again dance with joy, and plant and enjoy the produce.

Personal Application of the Principles: We, as believers, can be assured that God is faithful and loves us as He loves the people of Israel with an everlasting love and has drawn us to Himself with His steadfast and faithful loving-kindness. We can trust that God will restore us as well as the people of Israel. We need not worry that we must do so many works to be worthy of His love since we could never do enough, but God is the faithful One who loves us with an everlasting love.

Result: We can know God's everlasting love.

<u>Ask yourself:</u> How can I be assured of God's everlasting love even if I sin against Him?

How do I respond to God's faithfulness and His loving-kindness?

Day 39 ~ Walk by Faith

Read 2 Corinthians 5:1-10

2 Cor. 5:7 *"...for we walk by faith, not by sight..."*

Goal: To walk by faith

Obstacles: Unbelief, preoccupation with earthly cares, and burdens

Affirmations: Paul explains that when believers die, we will receive a new body from God that our spirits would not be naked. God prepared us for eternal life and gave us His Holy Spirit as a pledge that He would bring it about. While we are alive on earth, we are absent from the Lord in heaven, although we would prefer to be at home with the Lord. We desire to be pleasing to Him since we all must appear before the judgment seat of Christ to be recompensed for the deeds, good or bad, done while alive on earth.

Personal Application of the Principles: Christians understand and believe that when we die, we will receive a new body from God that is eternal. We are assured that our spirits will not be aimlessly wandering about, but rather clothed in our new resurrection bodies, and we have the Holy Spirit as a pledge that God will bring it about. We know that faith pleases God, and without faith, it is impossible to please Him.

Result: We will walk by faith.

Ask yourself: How can I be certain my walk is dependent on faith and not on what I see?

Do I fear or am I confident to stand before the judgment seat of Christ and why is this so?

Day 40 ~ Be Transformed

Read Romans 11:33-12:2

Rom. 12:2 *"And do not be conformed to this world, but be transformed by the renewal of your mind, that by testing you may discern what is the will of God, what is good and acceptable and perfect."* (ESV)

Goal: To be transformed

Obstacles: Living according to the style of this present age, conformity to the world, and pride.

Affirmations: Paul writes of the immeasurable depth of God's wisdom and knowledge, and that His judgments and ways are unsearchable and unfathomable. We know that all things are from Him, to Him, and for Him. Because of this, we should present ourselves in true worship, being transformed by the renewal of our minds thereby, proving what is the good, and acceptable, and perfect will of God.

Personal Application of the Principles: The immeasurable depth of God's wisdom and knowledge is made known to us along with the truth that His judgments and ways are unsearchable and unfathomable. Therefore, we should not be conformed to the world, but rather be transformed by the renewal of our minds that by testing, we may discern what is the perfect will of God.

Result: We will be transformed in the renewal of our minds.

Ask yourself: What does it mean to me to be transformed by the renewal of my mind?

How do I discern the good and acceptable and perfect will of God?

"The Lord is my portion," says my soul. "Therefore, I have hope in Him."   Lamentations 3:24

Dear Lord, give me assurance and grant me the peace of God that surpasses all understanding that will keep my heart and my mind in Christ Jesus for You alone are the supplier of all my needs.

Meet the Author

Rita Kroon was born in Minneapolis, but raised in St. Paul, MN. She graduated from Sibley High School and received her AA degree in speech/ communications from Lakewood Comm. College.

She is an author, blogger, and literary critic. She has written devotionals, Bible studies, novels (contemporary and historical), inspirational books, a memoir, wildlife magazine articles, children's short stories, poetry, and a humorous newspaper column "Rita Raps it up." Rita is a women's Bible study group leader.

Her current works are in memory of her husband, Burt, and their daughter, Rene'. Rita has two other daughters, LaDawn and Shelly, and lives in Lexington, MN,

Other Books by Rita Kroon

Womanhood: Becoming a Woman of Virtue is an
interactive Bible study of eight women of the
Old Testament and is suitable for group or
individual setting. There is an in-depth
section for the woman who likes to linger in
the Word and a condensed section designed
for the woman on the go. The in-depth
section has five daily homework assignments
that require approximately twenty minutes of
study time per day to complete. The complete study is 40
weeks but can easily be divided into 5-week segments. Personal
application questions are at the end of each daily lesson. The
condensed section is an eight-week study. Participants gather
for a two-hour session and work together on completing the
weekly assignments, the discussion questions and the
application questions. There is no homework!
SBN: 9780989198554

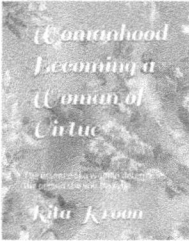

Cancer – a Journey through the Valley is a personal
memoir. Rita Kroon shares her journey
through the valley where she realized her faith
in God during the calm seasons of life
necessitated a mighty strengthening if it were
to sustain her on the battlefield.

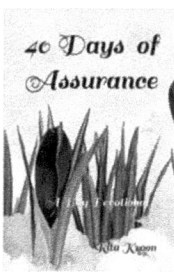

Discover how God worked such a faith while
she was in the throes of cancer. Be amazed at
the sovereignty of God to heal some and
stand in awe to see His grace given to those for whom He has
a different purpose.

ISBN: 9780989198516

Discover God through His Attributes is an inspirational guide to help in the search for a deeper and more meaningful relationship with God. Discover who He is. Be filled with awe. Give praise to the Lord of the heavens and the earth. Reverence Him for who He is, for there is no other god or anything in the entire universe like Him. Give Him the honor due to His holy name.

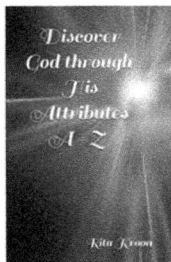

ISBN: 9780989198523

Kiss Your Mommy Goodbye is a Christian novel. Mike DiSanto and his wife, Lisa, are sinking in quicksand. Their four-year marriage ends in a courtroom, with full custody of their two-year old daughter, Maddy, awarded to Lisa. Mike is devastated, but Lisa stands tall like a princess, though she lost her kingdom. In his desperate quest to provide love and stability as a part-time father to Maddy, Mike does the unthinkable. He took a risk and lost. Mike learns that every choice has consequences as he struggles to reconcile and rebuild broken relationships. It is a story of hope, forgiveness, and peace with God and one another.

ISBN: 9780989198561

40 Days of Encouragement is a daily devotional that includes a goal set for each selection, the obstacles that may prohibit reaching your goal, and affirmations to help you overcome the hindrances to growing in your faith through personal application of the principles presented.

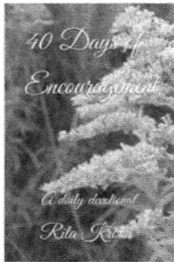

Drink deeply from God's word and be encouraged.

ISBN: **9780989198547**

40 Days in the Wilderness is a daily devotional with a goal set for each selected Scripture, the obstacles that often occur in daily life, and how to overcome the hurdles through personal application of the principles presented.

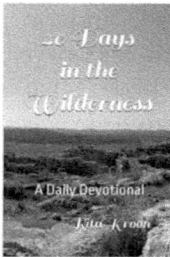

Come. Drink deeply from God's word and be refreshed.

ISBN: **9780989198509**

Praying the Scriptures is a collection of prayers and promises taken from God's Word, since no Word of God shall be void of power. When words cannot be found to say what is in your heart, this collection of prayers is meant to guide you through those moments of solitude. At other times when words to express your joy through praise and worship seem elusive, you can turn to the Scriptures.

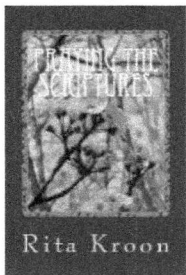

If praying may be unfamiliar, or has long ago been abandoned, Praying the Scriptures is one way to begin afresh. Discover the joy and power of prayer, and revel in the surety of His promises.

ISBN: 9780989198585

Nuggets from My Pocket is a collection of tidbits of wisdom, quotes, sayings, blessings, promises, and more that have been gathered along the trail. These gems of truth will inspire and encourage you. They will give you cause to pause, time to wonder and ponder and a reason to reflect. You will delight to share a nugget of encouragement with those around you.

Here's a nugget to ponder: "God gives evidence of His existence, but not proof since He always leaves room for faith."

ISBN: 9780989198592

More Nuggets from My Pocket is a collection of sayings, wit, insights, quotes, wisdom, promises, prayer, and more that were gathered where the trail led to an open meadow. These gems will inspire you and encourage you no matter what path of life you travel. Stop to ponder the insights given, or to discover a fresh perspective, or to glean new meaning to old sayings.

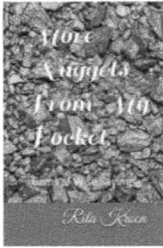

ISBN: 9798682187225

Extra Nuggets from My Pocket is a collection of sayings meant to stir your imagination, fill your heart, and satisfy your desire for fresh "Ah, moments."

Some of these gems of truth, wit, quotes, prayers, blessings, and more are mine and some are those I gathered along the way and tucked into my pocket.

ISBN: 9798587330566

Almost-Forgotten Nuggets is a collection of truthful, inspiring, and wise sayings, and follows the footprints of its three siblings, ***Nuggets from My Pocket, More Nuggets from My Pocket,*** and ***Extra Nuggets from My Pocket.*** The path is familiar, but the landscape has an added dimension of newness that makes the pleasant journey a most memorable one.

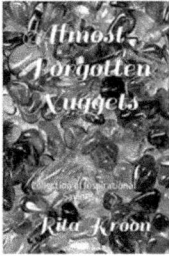

Here is a preview of what is inside - "Unconfessed sin is like a math problem: it divides the heart; adds woes; subtracts peace, and it multiplies consequences."   **ISBN: 9798511772042**

Letters from the Past is historical fiction. Through personal letters, eight women of Biblical times reveal their emotional impact of rape, infertility, incest, betrayal, and family dysfunction. They write of their trials and victories to the women of the twenty-first century, they also share their joy in overcoming seemingly impossible situations. One young woman risks her life when she is called to lead a nation. She responds with the brave words, "If I perish, I perish."

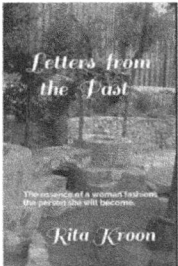

"Trial turns to triumph when the thread of God's faithfulness is traced through these authentic women from ancient times to today's woman. Suddenly there is no distance in time, no generational gap, and no heart left unturned. Today's woman will be challenged, filled with hope, and encouraged through the personal letters from Eve, Sarah, Rebekah, Rachel, Miriam, Deborah, Tamar, and Esther.   **ISBN: 9780989198578**

John – A Mini Study is a thirteen-week, interactive Bible study of the Gospel of John, and is suitable for individual or group setting. It uses an Observation-Interpretation-Application method of study in an easy-to-read format. One way to think of it is like this: The observation of facts is like reading a menu; the interpretation is looking at the number of calories or the price on the menu. Each application question is the main course – the most satisfying part of the meal that energizes us for action. Each lesson has a principle that helps to keep the participants focused on what the author is trying to convey. There are personal application questions and discussion questions to get the most out of studying God's Word.

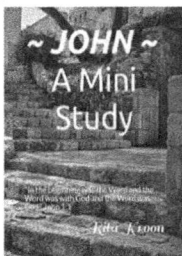

We learn what we can, apply what we know, and leave the rest to God.

"This is the disciple who testifies of these things and wrote these things, and we know this testimony is true." John 21:24 "BEHOLD! The Lamb of God!"

ISBN: 9798545633234

Pebbles of Truth is a collection of short, timeless sayings of truth that are filled with wisdom, give great insight, plus unforgettable quotes, encouragement, blessings, thoughts to remember, and explore God's greatness. These pebbles of truth connect the heart with one's imagination much like pebbles on a beach connect the water and the land.

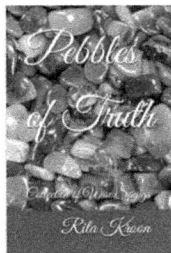

Here's a sneak peek: "Learn to write your hurts in the sand and to carve your blessings in stone." Here's another: "Man contributed nothing to his salvation except the sin that made it necessary."

ISBN: 9798842917037

A Walk to the Well

A Place for Women to find Encouragement, Hope, and Inspiration through the Blog, Books and Bible studies

www.awalktothewell.com